Writing Fiction: A Hands-On Guide for Teens

iUniverse books may be ordered through booksellers or by contacting:

iUniverse
1663 Liberty Drive
Bloomington, IN 47403
www.iuniverse.com
1-800-Authors (1-800-288-4677)

Because of the dynamic nature of the Internet, any Web addresses or links contained in this book may have changed since publication and may no longer be valid. The views expressed in this work are solely those of the author and do not necessarily reflect the views of the publisher, and the publisher hereby disclaims any responsibility for them.

ISBN: 978-1-4502-4069-7 (sc)
ISBN: 978-1-4502-4070-3 (ebook)

Printed in the United States of America

iUniverse rev. date: 6/28/2010

Writing Fiction:

A Hands-On Guide for Teens

Heather Wright

iUniverse, Inc.
New York Bloomington

This book is dedicated to my husband, my son, and my mom—with enormous thanks for their unrelenting support.

Acknowledgments

I'd like to thank my friend Jean for her ongoing encouragement and feedback. I'd like to thank the Storytellers for their support and the members of the Guelph and Waterloo Region branches of the Professional Writers Association of Canada for giving me the incentive to earn part of my living as a professional writer. I'd also like to thank Mike and Jean Leslie for giving me the chance to write the "Write Angles" column for *What If? Canada's Creative Teen Magazine*, which became the backbone of this book.

About Me (Or, The Page You Show the Parental Unit So That He or She Will Buy You the Book)

Why did I write this book? Because, like many writers, teachers, and editors, I believe in young writers. Young writers are capable, talented, and full of rich ideas for stories, and I love to be a part of those stories coming to life.

Here's some information about me. I am a teacher, currently teaching Communications at Conestoga College in Kitchener, Ontario, Canada. I taught high-school English for over fifteen years. I can analyze Shakespeare and parse a sentence with the best of them. I have a freelance writing business and write for the Web and for national and local publications. I was also awarded a Writers' Reserve Grant in 2010 by the Ontario Arts Council for a young adult novel in progress.

I love working with young writers and for four years had a how-to-write column in *What If? Canada's Creative Teen Magazine.* I taught a summer writing program at the art camp at the Homer Watson Gallery and have done school visits to talk about the life of a writer. I can't imagine my life without talking to young people about writing, watching them get motivated and empowered, and reading the great work that they produce.

I am a member of the Professional Writers Association of Canada and the Canadian Society for Children's Authors, Illustrators, and Performers and the Society for Children's Book Writers and Illustrator in the United States. You can check out the professional side of my writing life at ***www.wrightwriter.com.***

Please visit ***http://wrightingwords.wordpress.com***, which is the site dedicated to this book. There you will find updated links, blogs about the book, a place to just say "hello," and instructions for reaching me for virtual or in-person school visits and workshops.

Those are the bits you need to show the parental unit.

The rest is between you and me.

Between you and me, I love to write. Between you and me, the most fun I ever had as a teacher was in writing class. I love what young writers bring to the table. It inspires me, intimidates me, and makes me want to do my best work.

I'm hoping that my best work is this book, because I believe in you.

Contents

Introduction

I want to talk to you, writer to writer, about how you can write your best story possible. I want you to feel successful and professional and to have the tools that will help you write something that others will enjoy reading as much as you enjoyed writing. And I want to have some fun along the way.

This book is designed to hang around on your desk and be used whenever you're stuck on an aspect of writing or want to start a new project. I hope it's the start of a collection of books on writing that you will find at your local bookstore or borrow from the library.

The book does not contain a list of links to sites where young people can be published or to other writing references for young people. The reality is that these references will be out of date the moment I put them in print. For the most up-to-date links to publishers, resources, and anything else I think might be helpful, check my Web site: ***http://wrightingwords. wordpress.com.***

Setting Goals

What you choose to write is up to you, but setting goals is the best way to make sure that you get the story written. Experience also tells me that, even though I think I'm writing a short story, there's a very good chance that it will turn out to be a novel. So, keep in mind that goals can change.

The first thing you need to write is the first draft, and setting the goal to write that is the first step. The first draft is the playground when you were five years old and the rules of the games changed whenever you wanted the game to work better—or to give yourself a better chance to win. Your characters and imagination can change the rules—they can even change the game—but the goal is the same: finish the first draft. Without it, there is no story, no book, no series, no movie rights, no film premiere, no red carpet, no Oscar ... wait, that's my fantasy. It doesn't count as a goal.

Here's a sample of things that count as goals:

- I will write for twenty minutes every day.
- I will write two pages every day.
- I will finish my draft by my birthday.
- I will buy thirty copies of this book and give them to everyone in my class— oops—sorry! There goes my fantasy again.

If you like to write in your books, there's room on the next page to write your goals. I'm sure you have more than one story in you, so I've left lots of room for future goals, too.

My Goals

_____
_____
_____
_____
_____
_____
_____
_____
_____
_____
_____
_____
_____
_____
_____
_____
_____
_____
_____
_____
_____
_____
_____
_____
_____
_____
_____
_____
_____

Meeting Your Goals

Now that you've *set* your goals, what's next? Here are a few hints about how to achieve the goal of writing your first draft.

1.   Never make the deadline the deadline

If you've decided you will finish your draft in five weeks, move your deadline up a week, and give yourself only four weeks to complete the work. Lots of things can go wrong (aside from your own procrastination) to interfere with getting the draft done on time—computer problems, catching the flu, a major sports playoff that you just have to watch, your director calling an extra rehearsal, or a party invitation. So give yourself some breathing time, and achieve success.

2.   Set daily or weekly goals

If you've set a word-count or page-count goal, divide the total into manageable chunks, and the entire project will look a lot more attainable. I like to give myself weekly word-count goals and log my achievements on my calendar. If I exceed my goals, I definitely take a congratulatory trip to the coffee shop, but I don't use my success as an excuse to slack off on the next week's quota—besides, a café mocha is at stake!

3.   Make sure to allow time for research

Even if you're writing a children's story, there's bound to be some piece of information that you need to look up. For example, when, exactly, do kittens open their eyes? How tall is the average seven-year-old? And sometimes questions crop up as you write, or interesting tangents that you need to explore present themselves. If it looks like extensive research is in order, leave lots of blanks, or highlight the bits you need to research further, and move on. Unless it's a critical detail that's necessary for the plot to work or to move forward, you can do the rest of the research when the draft is finished, or when you're having a noncreative moment but want to keep working on your manuscript.

4.   Turn off the e-mail and MSN

You're a writer and your job is to write. People can wait to hear from you for a few hours and, yes, even days. Saying no to distractions honors both you and the work you are doing. For too short a time each day, writing is the most important job you have.

5.   Forgive yourself

If you don't make your quota, don't get frantic. Take a good look at your upcoming week and find the extra time you need to do the work. Then give yourself credit for being tough enough to get the job done.

Brain-Dump System

Now that you've set your goals, let's get on with the writing.

I'm going to assume that you have a story idea—in fact, you probably have more than one. With all the ideas churning in your brain, it's important to get them written down quickly before they get away.

Here's my "brain-dump" method of getting your ideas on paper and ending up with a story outline all at the same time.

Use the next page to write down all the events you picture happening in the story. You can start at the top and work your way down or turn the page and work side to side. It doesn't matter if the ideas come out in perfect order; we solve that problem later. It also doesn't matter whether the entire story is there or not. It's a good idea to leave one or two of the bubbles blank as you go along, too.

Maybe you only have a really clear picture of what happens in the first three chapters. Write those points down now. When you start writing your story, more of it will begin to unfold, and you can scribble those bits down as you start to see them, until you get to the conclusion—it's a sort of installment plan.

Maybe, like J. K. Rowling, you know the end of the story before you begin. That's what the bigger spaces at the bottom of the page are for. Most stories end with a big moment of excitement, where everything could go wrong, but finally has to go right for your main character (MC)—unless you're writing a tragedy, in which case everything will go wrong, and your MC will die to make life better for someone else.

When you've finished writing all your event ideas in the bubbles, take a pencil and start lightly drawing a line from the first bubble to the one you think should be next, and then to the next one, and so on. I suggested a pencil and a light line, because, as you move along, you may decide to change the order of things. You also may think of an event that needs to come between two that you already have, and that's where you can fill in those odd blank bubbles that you left the first time through—or scribble in between them, if you come up with a lot of ideas. For a small short story, you might not even need the entire page. For something longer, you might need a few pages to start.

When you've got things organized the way you like them, take a colored marker or pen and go over your pencil line. You now have the first plot plan for your story. I said "first" deliberately, because, if you're writing something long, like a novel, you'll want to go back and repeat this exercise as you move through your story. Somewhere between bubble seven and eight, you might come up with a wonderful idea that takes your MC in a different direction for a while. Do a shorter version of the brain dump to get those ideas in order, and then carry on.

I've put a few copies of this page in the book to get you started. You can always download a copy to print from my Web site at: ***http://wrightingwords.wordpress.com***

Brain Dump # __

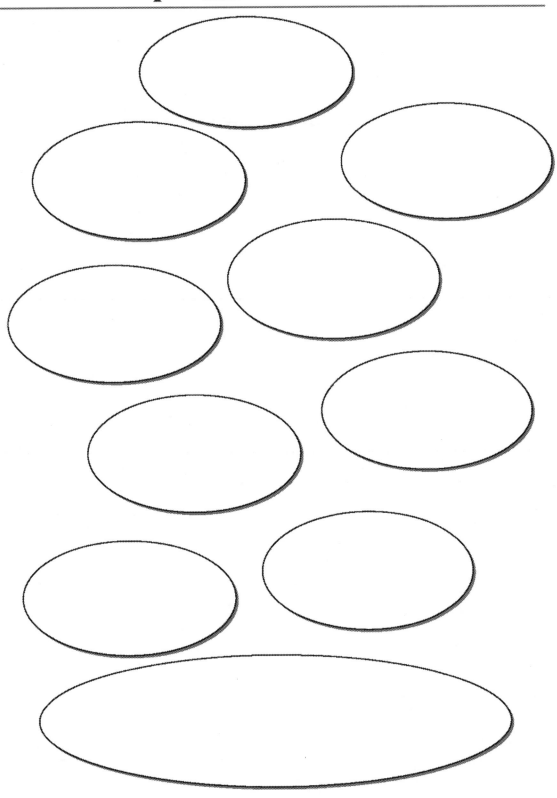

Brain Dump # __

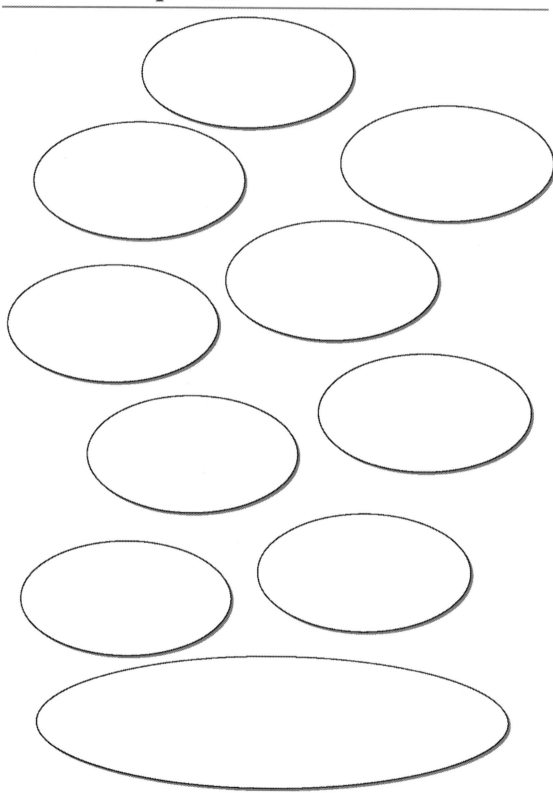

Brain Dump # __

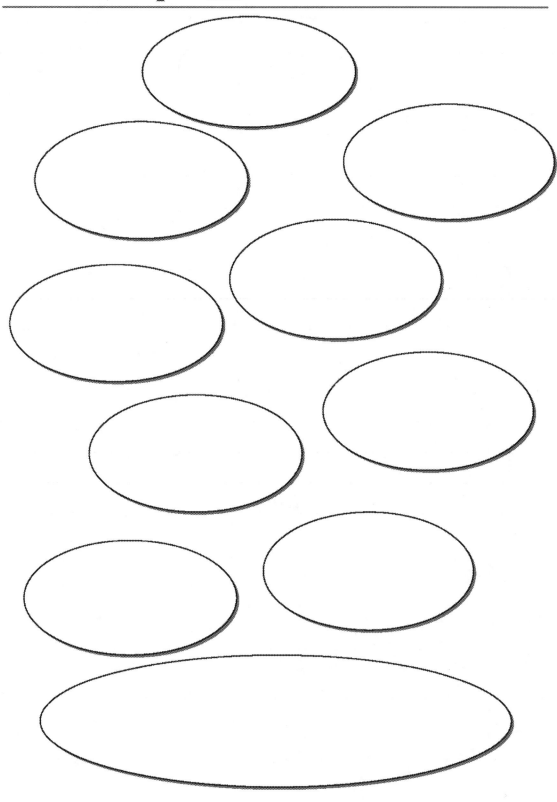

Brain Dump # __

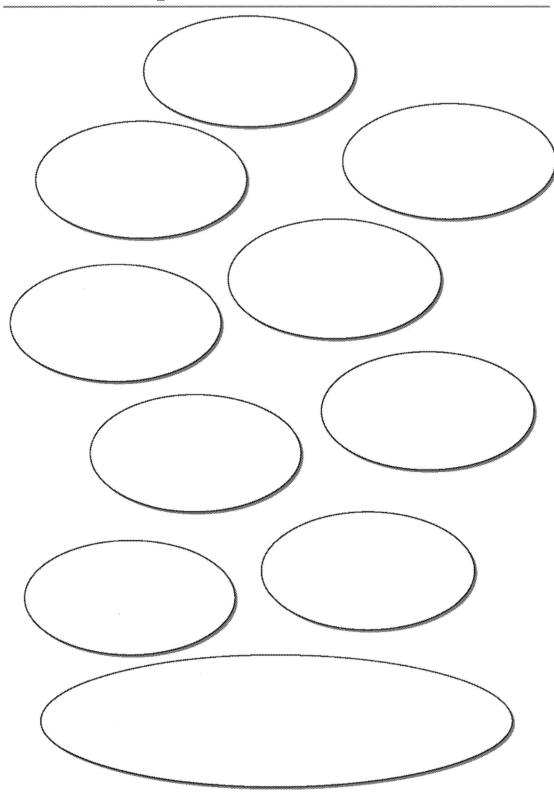

Brain Dump # __

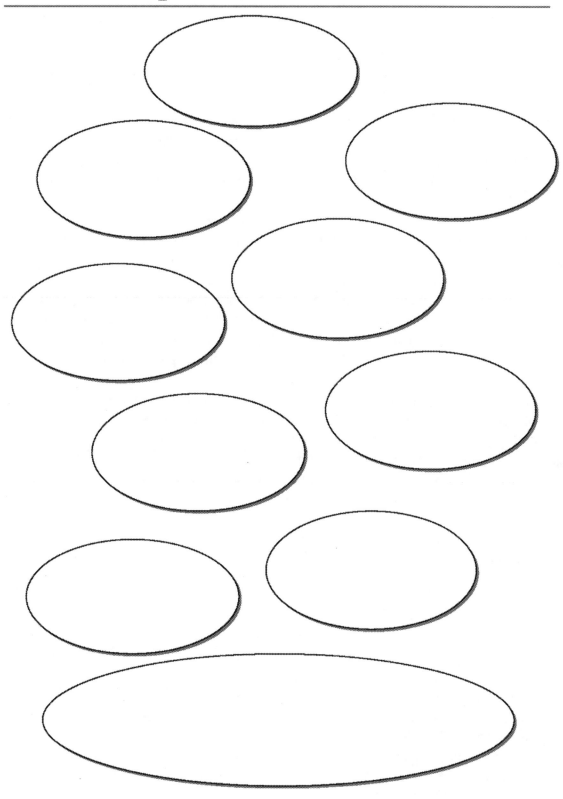

Stuck for a Story Idea?

Suggestion #1

You've heard the advice many times: "Write what you know." But, if you're like me, you thought, "Great, I can write about nothing—at least, nothing interesting." I mean, what kind of great novel was going to revolve around my ability at sixteen to pack a supermarket grocery bag, do homework, clean my room, listen to music with my friends, or sew my own clothes?

So, as I did with most advice that I didn't like, I ignored it—sort of.

Then I sat down and wrote a list of what I did know. And it turned out to be a much longer list than I thought it would be. I knew what it was like to be the slowest runner in the class, to wear glasses to school for the first time, and to stand in front of a group and tremble my way through a speech. I also knew what it felt like to pass my driver's test, have my tonsils out, and cook an edible Christmas dinner when my mom was sick.

I suggest that you create a *What-I-Know List*, too. Write down even the most insignificant things, because you never know when they will come in handy in a story. Ever fallen off a bike? Sure. But have you done it while being chased by the police, or a monster, or an angry crowd? You know what it's like to get up off the pavement, shaky and bleeding, and try to get back on the bike and ride home. Add those sensations of pain and the uncontrollable shakiness to the fear of the chase, and you can write a great scene!

As you write your list, think about the places you have visited: your aunt's farm, your sister's dorm room, the park, or the mall. Think about the places that you know the sight, smell, and sound of. Have you been to camp? Do you ski, or paint, or fish, or play sports? Do you play an instrument, or chess, or card games? Can you cook a meal, pitch a tent, take great photos, or dance?

All of these places and experiences open doors to stories. Your list provides you with a series of settings in which to place characters and then give them lots of trouble. A city-bred teenager and his six-year-old country cousin have to deliver a calf, because the uncle's truck has broken down on the way back from town. A campsite is washed out during a thunderstorm, and the guide is knocked unconscious by a falling branch. Your character's best friend steals a sweater from the mall. You know all the details about these locations, and you know what it's like to want to look cool in a situation in which you feel totally lost, or to be frightened, or to have your friendship tested.

A better way to phrase those famous words of advice might be, "Write what you know, and then grow!" Take an experience you've had and play with it; stretch it into something fresh and exciting by combining memory and imagination.

Write about what you want to know, too. I love medieval history, so I set a mystery for middle readers in England in the year 1214. I had great fun doing the research, because I knew I could use it for my story. I'm sure Christopher Paolini has never flown or known a dragon, but he wrote *Eragon* anyway, because he understood friendship and accepting challenges and being scared, and he made his dragons and the world they lived in just as real as all those things.

"Write what you know" isn't bad advice, but it's only a part of the package. Making a list and finding out that you really do know about a lot of things is a great first step. Adding imagination, emotions, and characters in conflict is the final step to creating your next great story. So, go ahead, make your list, and then write what you know—sort of.

My What-I-Know List

_____

_____

_____

_____

_____

_____

_____

_____

_____

_____

_____

_____

_____

_____

_____

_____

_____

_____

_____

_____

_____

_____

_____

_____

_____

_____

_____

_____

Suggestion #2

Use the following lists of words to create your own random writing prompts to help you come up with stories. From each twenty-six-word list, pick a number between one and twenty-six; that will be the number of the word that you will use from that column. When you've chosen four words, you'll have your writing challenge for the day. If there's someone around, ask him or her to pick the numbers for you.

airplane	cup	key	silver
airport	danger	knife	sleep
alien	desk	luck	slide
amulet	dog	match	spell
apple	doll	medal	spider
armour	door	minstral	spring
attack	dragon	monster	stone
bear	dream	mountain	string
blue	DVD	nail	summer
book	fall	needle	sword
boots	fear	paper	team
bracelet	field	peanut	team
brown	fire	pencil	thread
bulb	flame	phone	throne
bully	fortress	popcorn	thunder
camera	game	power	unicorn
cape	ghost	rain	wart
castle	glass	red	watch
cat	glue	ring	water
cave	gold	robe	weapon
chain	green	robin	window
chair	hat	sail	winter
charm	hero	scroll	witch
computer	hilt	ship	worm
copper	horse	shock	yarn
crystal	hut	shoe	yellow

Here's an example: 1, 7, 26, and 15 = airplane, dragon, shoe, thunder. During a thunderstorm, a plane makes an emergency landing. The survivors find themselves in a horseshoe-shaped valley in a deserted mountain range, where they find a family of dragons. Now, see what you can do!

Who, What, Where, When

Who: Your Characters

A rule about characters is to know wa-a-a-a-y more about them than you tell your reader. You can find out about them in a few ways.

One way is to create the classic character sketch. Lots of writers (and teachers) have their own versions of these, but here is mine. I've put a few more at the end of this section for you to work with. You can download more at *http://wrightingwords.wordpress.com*. If your story has a villain, make sure to spend the same amount of time on him or her as on your main character (MC).

Character's Name: _____

Physical Description: _____

_____

_____

_____

Attitude:
- Toward life _____

  _____

- Toward friends _____

  _____

- Toward family _____

  _____

- Toward school/work _____

  _____

Two secrets that the character hasn't told anyone: _____

_____

_____

_____

_____

One thing that frightens the character: _____

_____

One internal conflict that the events or the emotions in the story make worse or force the character to overcome:

_____

_____

_____

Other neat things about my character:

_____

_____

_____

_____

_____

_____

Here's a sample for a character you might know in the first book of this well-known series.

Character's Name: Harry Potter

Physical Description:

- skinny
- black hair
- lightning-shaped scar on forehead
- clothes too big

Attitude:

- Toward life: Life is pretty ugly at the moment. He's just trying to make it from day to day without being bullied by Dudley.

- Toward friends: He wishes he had some.

- Toward family: He wonders what his parents were like and wishes they were still alive. He wishes his aunt and uncle didn't hate him so much.

- Toward school/work: He doesn't mind it; he's an okay student. School is a distraction from the Dursleys. He's glad Dudley's going away to school, so he won't have to see him for months at a time.

Two secrets that the character hasn't told anyone: He can make things happen that he can't explain. He can talk to snakes.

One thing that frightens the character: He's afraid he's not normal, because weird things happen sometimes, and he thinks he must cause them.

One internal conflict that the events or the emotions in the story make worse or force

Of course, Harry's internal conflict is partly solved when he goes to Hogwarts, because he is finally among people who are wizards, too. Unfortunately, Harry is a special wizard, with special powers, who defeated Voldemort while only a baby. This special ability, over which Harry had no control, still makes him an outsider trying to belong. He would love to be just like everyone else. Realizing that he can never be like everyone else and that he will have to follow a different path than everyone else is a conflict that he faces many times throughout the entire series of books.

Another way to help you visualize your characters is to cut pictures of them out of magazines or catalogues and post them on the wall above your desk. Attach sticky notes to them with important details like eye color, height, age, etc. It's easy to forget that you gave your character blue eyes in Chapter 1 when you have her true love gazing into her violet eyes in Chapter 7.

A third way to learn about your characters is to interview them. Pretend you are a journalist for your MC's local newspaper or a gossip magazine, and interview your MC about his or her life or goals or how he or she got into this particular situation. Make yourself a very unlikeable reporter who asks all the hard and embarrassing questions, and see what your character comes up with.

One caution: The reader doesn't need to know everything you know. There's nothing that turns a reader off more than an information dump by the author that neither moves the plot along nor reveals anything important about the MC. If you've decided that your character absolutely loves chocolate truffles, there's no point in telling the reader that piece of information—unless, somewhere in the story, your character's inability to resist chocolate truffles affects the plot.

Character Sketch

Character's Name: _____

Physical Description: _____

_____

_____

_____

Attitude:
- Toward life _____

  _____

- Toward friends _____

  _____

- Toward family _____

  _____

- Toward school/work _____

  _____

Two secrets that the character hasn't told anyone: _____

_____

_____

_____

_____

One thing that frightens the character: _____

_____

One internal conflict that the events or the emotions in the story make worse or force the character to overcome:

_____

_____

_____

Other neat things about my character:

_____

_____

_____

_____

_____

_____

Character Sketch

Character's Name: _____

Physical Description: _____
_____
_____
_____

Attitude:
- Toward life _____
_____

- Toward friends _____
_____

- Toward family _____
_____

- Toward school/work _____
_____

Two secrets that the character hasn't told anyone: _____
_____
_____
_____
_____

One thing that frightens the character: _____
_____

One internal conflict that the events or the emotions in the story make worse or force the character to overcome:
_____
_____
_____

Other neat things about my character:
_____
_____
_____
_____
_____
_____

Seasons Change and So Should Your Characters

Many stories follow a similar pattern. At the beginning of the story, the main character believes that the world works in one particular way. After experiencing challenges, dangers, discoveries, or losses, the main character realizes that the world works differently, and he either learns how to accept and live in this new world or how to change it. If it's a tragedy, the hero may die so that others can live better lives in this newly realized world.

This description applies to characters as seemingly different as Frodo, Luke Skywalker, Scout Finch, and the Grinch. The theme that makes all of these characters worth following through a book or film (or a series of books or films) is the theme of change—of beginning the story with one set of abilities or beliefs and ending the story with new ones.

Frodo changes because he learns what evil, courage, and friendship really are. Luke Skywalker learns how to use the force and to trust that there is good in a person that others have given up on. Scout Finch learns how to see the world through someone else's eyes. And the Grinch learns to love others more than himself.

Would we reread these books or watch these films again and again if these characters had learned nothing? No. Readers and viewers love the moment when the character must pass the test of change. All the events of the films and the books lead to the moment when the characters' experiences give them the insight needed to make that final choice. This choice could not have been made wisely by the character who began the story, but it can be trusted in the hands of the person the character has become after a novel or film full of challenges and conflict.

Rowling's Harry Potter series is a wonderful example of how change and dealing with change link the events of a story and develop character. Harry Potter lives a life of isolation, maltreatment, and low self-esteem at the hands of his aunt and uncle—until his eleventh birthday, when he discovers that he is really a wizard with magic powers.

Though this magic frees him, temporarily, from his horrible home life, it also brings with it great danger. Harry is the one person that the greatest evil wizard of all time will stop at nothing to destroy. The change in Harry's circumstances is brought about by an outside source: a letter of invitation to Hogwarts School is delivered with great persistence by the giant, Hagrid. Harry suddenly has new clothes, money, and an explanation for some strange things that have happened to him, but there are internal changes that need to take place, too.

Harry needs to understand his magical powers, accept the new knowledge of his parents' murders, and cope with being a celebrity after his unconscious defeat of Voldemort while an infant. He needs to survive Voldemort's revenge and, elsewhere in his life, make friends, deal with bullies, play Quidditch, and pass exams. In every new novel, Rowling adds to Harry's challenges, and Harry grows and learns how to overcome them. Conflict and character are intertwined, so that one builds upon the other.

Clearly, conflicts that are less life threatening can still result in meaningful changes for the characters in your stories. Perhaps your character learns who his friends really are after nearly losing them through being selfish or trying to impress someone who really wasn't worth it. Maybe your character loses a friend or a pet and learns how to deal with her grief by helping others deal with theirs or learns the value of memory or the need to value every day as it comes. Whatever conflicts your characters endure, make sure they learn something from the experience that makes them see and, perhaps, live their lives differently.

Look at your stories and characters in terms of change. What challenges are you giving your characters, and how are they changing to overcome them? Maybe, in some way, their hearts grow bigger, or their empathy for others is developed, or their self-confidence grows, or their ability to wield special powers increases and leads them to further challenges (and a sequel!).

Whatever you choose for your characters, make sure you also choose change.

What: Your Plot

What happens to your character is what makes your plot. One example of a surefire plot is the concept of the "hero's journey." You may have been taught this in school, but, if not, the short explanation is that it's derived from the work of Joseph Campbell. He studied stories from around the world, ancient legends, myths, and the work of great writers of the past. He realized that, throughout all the world's cultures, one story pattern could be found, and that was the hero's journey—and it's a pattern that is still used today. Two great books on the subject, written especially for writers, are *The Writer's Journey: Mythic Structure for Writers,* by Christopher Vogler and *The Key: How to Write Damn Good Fiction Using the Power of Myth,* by James N. Frey.

The hero's journey follows a pattern similar to the one below. If you check the Internet, you'll find lots of examples of hero's journey outlines. Read the following version, and, if you're a Harry Potter fan, think of how the pattern fits his story.

- The hero has an "unusual" birth. Often the hero is an orphan or has something mysterious in his past.
- The hero is asked to do something out of his or her comfort zone and initially refuses. Then the hero is asked again, but this time he or she decides to accept.
- Early in the journey, the hero gets help from someone wise.
- The hero travels from the familiar world to the adventure world.
- The hero is tested by people and events.

- The hero often has a helper or sidekick in the adventure world.
- The hero faces a final battle where all could be won or lost.
- After the battle, the hero returns with something that benefits others.
-

Not every element of your story has to match exactly the list above, but it is a tried-and-true storytelling pattern that has pleased readers and audiences for thousands of years. Here's how it works in two movies you might know.

Hero's Journey in *Transformers* and *Princess Diaries*

Characteristic	Example from *Transformers*	Example from *Princess Diaries*
The hero has an "unusual" birth. Often the hero is an orphan or has something mysterious in his past.	Sam Witwicky has a great-great grandfather who was an explorer and went mad. Sam is an outsider at school.	Mia lives with her mom and doesn't know the truth about her father. She is an outsider at school.
The hero is asked to do something out of his or her comfort zone and initially refuses. Then The hero is asked again, but this time he or she decides to accept.	Sam realizes his car is unusual when he sees it transform, but he doesn't want to know more at first. Later, he encourages Mikaela to get in the car to find out more about what is going on.	Mia goes to visit her grandmother and learns about her father. She never wants to see her grandmother again. Later she agrees to take "princess lessons."
Early in the journey, the hero gets help from someone wise.	Sam's car helps him spend the day with Mikaela. Later, it helps them both escape the police car.	Mia is befriended by Joseph, head of security.
The hero travels from the familiar world to the adventure world.	Sam meets Optimus Prime and the rest of the autobots and learns about Megatron's evil plans. He agrees to help the autobots.	Mia spends time at the embassy with the queen, learning how to be a princess.
The hero is tested by people and events.	Sam has to lie to his parents, cope with the police and the government agents, rescue Bumblebee, and erase Mikaela's criminal record.	Mia has a disastrous debut at an embassy dinner, is tricked at a beach party, and nearly loses her friends.

The hero often has a helper or sidekick in the adventure world	Sam is befriended by Optimus Prime. Mikaela is also his helper.	Once Mia tells her secret, her friend supports her.
The hero faces a final battle where all could be won or lost.	Sam, Michaela, the soldiers, Optimus Prime, and the autobots defeat Megatron	Mia upsets her friends, and she wants to run away. She realizes she has to say she is sorry and live up to her responsibilities, after she reads her father's diary.
After the battle, the hero returns with something that benefits others.	Optimus Prime says, "We are in your debt." For the moment, the battle has been won, and there will be peace.	Mia agrees to accept her role as princess, and the kingdom is saved.

Where and When: Your Setting

There is one thing that you need to remember about your setting, whether it's on the moon, in your cousin's school, or in a land and time far, far away—it needs to be tangible. Your setting needs to have all the dimensions of sight, taste, hearing, touch, and smell, and it needs to affect your characters and the plot.

If your plot is set in a high school, then the daily life of your characters is filled with the regular ringing of class changes and loudspeakers, by the smells of wet winter clothes, gym change rooms, and cafeteria mystery meat. Texture comes from sticky cafeteria tables and broken chairs that pinch the backs of your legs when you least expect it. You don't have to describe every aspect of high school life, because your readers will have some idea of what it's about from their own experience or from seeing it in movies and TV. Some small, vivid reminders of the parts of high school that aren't just seen will give your readers that moment when they can fall more deeply into the life of your characters and the world they inhabit.

It's even more important to provide concrete details when your setting is more exotic and not one that your readers will likely have inhabited themselves. Science fiction and fantasy need a careful touch. You don't want to drown your readers in details—but think about the ones that are essential to your character and his or her actions. You might have a situation where your character curses the extra bright light provided by two moons while he's trying to break into the enemy's camp, and the extraordinarily high and low tides caused by the moons add complications when his escape is delayed.

One way to make your story's setting come to life is to draw a map of the locations of your story. Even if your setting is a thinly disguised rendition of your own neighborhood, drawing a map is a good way to open doors to some things you might not have thought of. What is beyond the two blocks that surround your MC's house? Who lives there? Is it someone who has just moved in and could shake up the story and your characters a bit? Keep drawing your map in ever-widening circles, until you are on Main Street or at the mall, and be open to what might decide to arrive on the page. Maybe there's a blank space you can't figure out how to fill, and then you realize it's a cemetery with a freshly dug grave and one small bouquet of flowers. Maybe it's an abandoned lot that has remained empty for thirty years, since the house on it burned down; no one even walks across it for a shortcut. Maybe, it's a portal to another universe.

Drawing the map isn't an exercise in being a good artist but, rather, an exercise in building a world that you can confidently walk your character around—without finding out on page thirty-eight that you have him turning left into a mini-mall where on page three you'd created a park. The exercise serves a couple of purposes: letting your imagination work in a different way than with words, and mapping out a setting that will stay consistent through a longer work.

I also suggest drawing maps as a way to find a plot in the first place. Draw a detailed map of an imaginary town—or neighborhood or island or country or planet—and then imagine what could happen there. Who might live there and need to move from one place to another? Do the names you chose for streets, or mountains, or swamps suggest a mystery, a comedy, a fantasy, or a romance? Is the place you've created one where people fall in love, use magic, or fight evil androids?

Drawing provides an extra bonus, in that it connects to the right side of your brain and helps quiet the critical, linear left side, allowing your creativity to shine. Give it a try, especially if the voices in your head are particularly loud and rude about your writing talent today. Even taking some time to color a picture in your kid sister's coloring book can make all the difference.

Draw a map, rely on your senses, select your details carefully, and your setting will become that important other character in your story.

Ways to Start a Story

Imagine that you've just eavesdropped on the most amazing conversation, read the most bizarre article in the newspaper, or emerged from a dazzling daydream. Whatever your inspiration, a great story has magically materialized, screaming to get on paper. But how do you begin? Well, there isn't one answer to that question—there are three, and one of them will be the best one for the story *you* want to tell.

With Character

One choice is to get your main character on stage right away—or someone who is going to lead us to the MC. Your MCs are the reason you write stories. They have problems and must solve them; they have to learn and change. They need to resolve conflicts—internal and external—and then find peace in the universe, true love, and the cure for the common cold. In other words, these people have things to do, so get them "doing" early.

When your MC walks on stage in the first paragraph, have her acting, reacting, getting in trouble, running from trouble, or planning trouble. You can fill in later *how* she got to this point—once the reader is ready to take a pause in the action for a little enlightening dialogue or narrative.

Be wary of the story opening that spends a lot of time inside your protagonist's mind, especially if she's thinking back over all the things that happened to her before the moment when the reader meets her. The words "I remember when" can bring many readers to a halt. They've just met a character and want to know what's *ahead* for her in the pages to come, not what's *behind* her. But if your need to tell that story is strong, maybe your real story is the one about the actions and trouble your heroine has experienced to bring her to this point. Begin at *that* beginning, and see what happens.

With Action

An action scene is another starting strategy for your story. It sets the tone by bringing the reader vividly into the world that your characters inhabit. A street fight, a deadly battle with lasers or magic, a runaway train—all these set the scene for danger and adventure. A mystery novel might begin with the victim's murder. A suspense story about the uncovering of a blackmailer, or a drug dealer, or a corporate spy might begin with the car crash that sets the antagonist's evil plots unraveling. These are fun to write, but make sure that you get your hero into the story soon, so the reader knows through whose eyes he will be seeing the events unfold.

With Setting

Describing the setting is another way to start, but it comes with some words of caution. The first are "keep it short." Don't forget that description is the part of the story that *you* usually skip when you're reading! Your story opening has to be more than a weather report, too.

Look at Michael Crichton's opening to *Jurassic Park*. He uses violent language to describe a violent storm, with lots of noise, destructive wind, and rain. We see that nature is powerful, dangerous, and uncontrollable, just like the dinosaurs he writes about. He uses the description to effectively foreshadow the dangers that will follow in his novel and to set the mood of threat and imminent violence.

When you decide to use a setting description to begin your story, make sure that it does its share of foreshadowing and mood evocation, as well as painting a picture of where and when the story will take place. You're using space in your story that could be filled with a character, so make your description just as important and compelling as your hero is.

Setting, character, and action—these three story openings can hook your reader and get the pages turning. Experiment with them all, and find the one that feels just right for the story you have to tell. And remember that these methods don't have to be used in isolation.

Here's the opening of a current work in progress (WIP) that combines all three methods. The novel is an adventure fantasy for middle readers, and the opening paragraphs tell the readers right away that they're going to be sharing an adventure with a fourteen-year-old who has a fair share of attitude.

Remember, too, that the beginning of your story is the beginning of your commitment to the reader. Though your story beginning doesn't lay out the following content of your work as precisely as the first paragraph of a five-paragraph essay, it should, in hindsight, lead logically in tone, style, and content to the rest of your story. The opening below promises action—I'd better make sure I deliver just that over the next seventy thousand words, or I'll have broken that commitment to my reader.

> *"Okay. I'm going!" My voice seemed to echo in the empty street, as the door slammed behind me. No surprise. It was the first day of summer vacation, and all the other kids were in their pajamas watching TV or playing video games. But not me. I was running to the store for milk—and it wasn't even nine o'clock yet! My typical luck.*
>
> *I veered off the sidewalk where the path led down the hill through the woods. The store was in the mini-mall opposite my school, and the hydro corridor that ran through our subdivision went right behind it.*

I didn't get that far. My ankle caught on something in the path and I was base over apex and flat on my butt in a millisecond. "Crap!" Could things get worse? The pain shot from my ankle to my gut and back again. What had I run into? It definitely hadn't been on this path before. I'd run down here hundreds of times.

I got up and limped back to see what it was. It looked like just a lump of dirt. When I pushed it with my foot, some of the dirt scraped off. Whatever it was wasn't moving. I knelt down and pulled away the damp soil and grass around it—and decided I must be nuts.

I couldn't see anyone coming, so I started digging—fast—and throwing dirt everywhere. I looked around again, while I wiped my muddy hands on the grass. No one.

I braced myself and pulled. It took three tries, but finally I was standing holding a sword. I waited. Absolute silence, and then I felt like an idiot. It wasn't as if crowds of people were going to suddenly appear and make me king of England or something. Excalibur had been stuck in a stone in a fairy tale, not in a dirt path in Kitchener, Ontario, Canada. This was still pretty weird, though.

I passed it back and forth between my hands, seeing how it balanced and checking its weight. This thing was definitely no toy. It was nearly half a kilo heavier than the swords in kung fu class, and even though it was covered in dirt, I could tell it was deadly. But what was it doing here? I looked around to see if anyone could see, and then I took some experimental swings and feinted with a nearby tree.

The sword felt as if it were a part of me—as if I'd been born to hold it. My whole body felt energized and strong. The feeling vanished almost as soon as I started enjoying it. Mom would kill me when I brought it home.

Here's a second example, from a WIP for which I received a Writers' Reserve grant from the Ontario Arts Council. Though the action only consists of fighting with a school lock, it's enough action to give my character an early conflict to face. How she handles it, and what she's thinking while she deals with it, tell the reader more about my MC.

I was totally fed up, and then Shawn came along.

Starting a new school sucked. For the entire Labor Day weekend, I had been putting on a brave face for my little brother, keeping cheerful in front of my mom at the hospital, and reassuring my dad that it was okay for Mike and me to live in town with Auntie Isobel while mom was sick. Today, I'd spent the morning trying not to look like a total loser as I walked down all the wrong halls at Central Wilton High School. Now I was hungry, fighting with my lock combination for the third time, and ready to throw my books out the nearest window—if, in this prison of a new school, there was one that even opened.

"Hi. Can I help?"

I looked up and saw the guy I'd sat beside in history class. If Justin Timberlake had a secret twin, this guy was it—except this guy had blue eyes.

"My lock won't open," I said, wishing I still had even a bit of lip gloss left on.

"Can I try? I promise, if you give me your combination, I will definitely forget it. I keep mine written in my student agenda." He paused and smiled. "I can guarantee I'll remember your name, though."

I smiled back. "I'm Lacey." I handed him the sticker that had come with my lock.

"I'm Shawn," he said and then released my lock with three quick twists of the dial. He opened my locker door for me and bowed. "Here you go, my lady."

I couldn't help but smile. It was the first smile I'd actually felt in days. "Thanks," I said. I dumped my books inside and grabbed my lunch.

"Do you have anyone to eat with?" he asked.

Things were getting better! "No. I don't know anyone here."

"No problem," he said. " I'll introduce you to some people. Wait here; I'll get my lunch and be right back." He walked down the long hall and turned the corner.

I was scrambling in my purse for lip gloss, when a voice said quietly behind me, "Hi. This is my locker."

"Oh, sorry." I moved out of the way.

"I'm Josh; I saw you in history this morning."

Obviously the teacher had been as boring as I'd thought he was, if these guys had both had the time to notice me. Josh was just a little taller than me, with a great smile, lots of messy blond hair, and an AC/DC T-shirt.

"You want to have lunch together?" he asked.

"Oh. I ... um ... Shawn asked me. I'm just waiting for him."

Josh's smile disappeared. "Shawn is trouble. I can't tell you anymore now. But stay away. He's not just trouble; he's dangerous." He turned away and started restacking the books in his locker.

I want the reader to identify with Lacey and be on her side early in the story. It's very soon for readers to care about her and her actual fate, but they've got a been-there-done-that identification with her right away. I hope that that early identification helps them start the relationship with her that I want to see last until the end of the novel.

Dialogue

Three rules about dialogue—my rules, of course, so keep this in perspective

Rule 1

IGNORE THE POSTER THAT'S BEEN IN YOUR CLASSROOM SINCE DAY ONE THAT LISTS ALL THE WORDS YOU CAN USE INSTEAD OF *SAID*.

Guess what? *Said* is just fine, and there are a lot better ways of making dialogue and characters interesting than having characters cajole, whimper, whine, exclaim, hiss, etc. Dialogue's purpose is to tell your reader more about your character, and there are better ways to do it.

Here's a for-instance: *"Help!" Vikki exclaimed.* This is a perfectly good sentence, but it doesn't tell us much about Vikki. And, besides, since the word *help* is followed by an exclamation mark, it's redundant to say that she *exclaimed*. Here's another example, which tells us a little more about Vikki. *"Help!" Vikki prided herself on never raising her voice, but she yelled now.*

Sometimes you don't even have to use the word *said*. Once you identify which one of the two people in your dialogue starts first, the rest is easy. As long as you start a new paragraph every time a new person speaks, the reader can keep track of who is saying what just fine.

For example:

> *"You're late," said Jim.*

> *"You need to get a new watch," said Bill. "I'm on time."*

> *"Okay. Doesn't matter. Did you bring it?"*

> *"I couldn't. My dad was watching me."*

> *"Well, thanks for nothing."*

> *"I did bring this, instead."*

> *"Cool."*

You know that Jim is the last person to speak, without the *said*s.

Rule 2

DIALOGUE ISN'T REMOTELY REALISTIC.

Can you imagine reading the following and being even a little interested?

> *Ginny met Leon at their usual meeting place in the music room.*
>
> *"Hi," said Ginny. "How're you doing?"*
>
> *"Great. How are you?" said Leon*
>
> *"I think I'm getting a cold."*
>
> *"Oh, I hope not."*
>
> *"Me, too."*
>
> *"Did you hear about Mike?"*
>
> *"No. What happened?"*
>
> *"Well, I heard he was—zzzzzzzzzzzzzzzzzzzzzzzzzzzz."*

People talk like that, but writers don't write like that, or they'd lose their readers in words that fill space but don't move the story along.

Here's another try at the same thing:

> *Ginny met Leon at their usual meeting place in the music room.*
>
> *"Leon, did you hear about Mike? He's been suspended."*

Much better. We have cut to the chase, and now we are ready to see how Leon will react to Ginny's news.

Rule 3

DIALOGUE ISN'T JUST TALKING; IT'S ABOUT ACTION AND CHARACTER.

Dialogue is the perfect place for you to describe what your characters are doing. It helps the readers understand them better, hear them better, and see them better.

Let's put Ginny and Leon back in the music room and see what happens.

> *Ginny and Leon met in their usual meeting place in the music room.*
>
> *Ginny had a wicked gleam in her eyes that Leon recognized right away. She had a juicy piece of gossip that she couldn't wait to tell.*
>
> *"Leon, did you hear about Mike? He's been suspended."*
>
> *"What!" Leon stepped back and knocked over all the music stands for the flute section. "Oh, crap," he said, scrambling to put the stands back where they belonged.*
>
> *"What's the matter with you?" Ginny watched him, with her hands on her hips and her head to one side.*
>
> *Leon didn't like that look. Did she know he was going to be next?*

There are no *exclaim*s (even though Leon does just that), *said*s, *asked*s, or anything else from the list. But we can hear their voices, see them, and know more about what makes them tick—because we see their physical actions, reactions, and, in Leon's case, hear what the character is thinking.

This leads to a discussion of point of view, so that's the next chapter.

Point of View

In the last chapter, you read a short scene between Ginny and Leon, which was told from Leon's point of view. We were inside his head, and we saw and heard Ginny's comments with Leon's eyes and ears.

One of the early things you need to decide when you start writing your story or novel is whose voice you are going to use to tell the story. It's a decision that, once made, you need to stick to for the balance of the story. I could just have easily decided to describe the scene in the last chapter from Ginny's point of view. It might have read like this:

> *Ginny and Leon met in their usual meeting place in the music room.*
>
> *Ginny knew she gave it away when she had some juicy gossip to tell. Usually, her friends couldn't wait to hear her news, but Leon looked more like someone who was going to have a tooth drilled than someone who was about to hear the latest news.*
>
> *"Leon, did you hear about Mike? He's been suspended." She'd thought it was a pretty good bit of news, but she hadn't expected Leon's reaction. Not one bit.*
>
> *"What!" Leon stepped back and knocked over all the music stands for the flute section. "Oh, crap," he said, scrambling to put the stands back where they belonged.*
>
> *"What's the matter with you?" Leon looked scared, and Ginny couldn't wait to find out why.*

Both the Ginny/Leon sets of dialogue use a point of view called "third person limited." We are limited to the thoughts of one person, but the description of Leon's actions in knocking over the music stands come from the author.

If this scene were written in "third person omniscient," we would be able to get inside both Ginny and Leon's heads, and the scene might read like this. This style can be wordier and it can be harder to decide which character the reader is supposed to care about more.

> *Ginny and Leon met in their usual meeting place in the music room.*
>
> *Ginny had a wicked gleam in her eyes that Leon recognized right away. She had a juicy piece of gossip that she couldn't wait to tell.*

Ginny knew she gave it away when she had some juicy gossip to tell. Usually, her friends couldn't wait to hear her news, but Leon looked more like someone who was going to have a tooth drilled than someone who was going to hear the latest news.

"Leon, did you hear about Mike? He's been suspended." She'd thought it was pretty good bit of news, but she hadn't expected Leon's reaction. Not one bit.

"What!" Leon stepped back and knocked over all the music stands for the flute section. Oh, crap," he said, scrambling to put the stands back where they belonged.

"What's the matter with you?" Leon looked scared, and Ginny couldn't wait to find out why.

Leon didn't like the way Ginny watched him, with her hands on her hips and her head to one side. Did she know he was going to be next?

Another way to handle various points of view in the same story is to limit each chapter to one point of view rather than bounding from head to head in the same chapter. It's a lot easier for the reader to find and accept the pattern of what the writer is doing.

A very popular point of view is first person. This has advantages and a couple of challenges. The advantage is that first person provides the writer with an excellent tool to bring the reader right inside the character. It provides the author the opportunity to add humor by juxtaposing the character's thoughts against what he or she is saying or appearing to be in the story. Here's an example. Wyatt has just found a sword on a path behind his house and gone to the creek to wash the dirt off.

"And just what do you think you are doing?" demanded a female voice from the other side of the creek.

I looked up and saw three things: a girl, around sixteen, with long, red hair and an attitude; behind her, where Broad Hill subdivision was supposed to be, a large quilt of small cultivated fields; and, on the hill beyond them, a castle.

Giga-crap! What the blazes was going on? I gripped the hilt of the sword as tightly as I could and then released my hand. My palm was marked with indentations, red against my white skin. I couldn't be dreaming. But then, what?

The girl spoke again. "Are you going to kneel there gawking, boy, or are you going to get back to your wagon?"

"To my what?" I could barely hear her over the pounding of my heart. I looked around for something, anything, familiar. Nothing. I stood up slowly. I had that scary tremble in my knees I only ever felt in Principal Forman's office—and that never went well.

"Who are you?" I tried to keep my voice from doing the stupid squeak it did when I was nervous. I failed. Where on earth was I, and where did that castle come from?

The girl squinted at me, shook her head, and then spoke again. She pronounced every word very slowly, as if I were a total moron, "You are with the actors, are you not?"

She sounded like no one else I'd ever heard. It was English of some kind, but the words were pronounced differently. At least it was English. Now, just what did she mean by "actors"?

"Surely you do not pretend to be a knight, dressed as foolishly as you are?"

Now she was talking about knights! And as for dressing foolishly, she'd already won first prize. She looked like some hippie from the sixties, with her dress dragging on the ground, her long hair, and her boots.

She took a few steps farther along the bank, so she was nearly opposite me. "Is that sword for the play tonight?"

"Um ... yeah ... sure." Whatever you say, lady. This was no time to annoy a lunatic—or did I mean another lunatic? I ran my hand over my head, looking for lumps. I must have hit my head, and I'm hallucinating. Whatever was going on, I needed to get to somewhere I recognized—and soon.

A challenge of writing in first person is that it does limit your reader to knowing only what the MC knows. You can't write about, and the reader can't discover, what is happening in anyone else's head except the MC's. This means, of course, that the MC can assume all sorts of things about the motives of those he or she interacts with, leaving the reader, who takes a slightly more distanced view, to judge whether those assumptions are correct or not. This technique can create more humor and can also add suspense if the reader sees that the MC's assumption is dangerously off-track, but the MC insists on following that assumption anyway.

Keep in mind, too, that it's not always easy to pick the right POV for your story or novel right away. It may take a few tries. I started the first draft of a fantasy novel in third person limited, and by the time I was in chapter three, I had changed to first person and just kept on going. I'll go back and change the beginning when I've finished the first draft. This experience is all part of the playground that first drafts represent. I changed the rules to suit the game I wanted to play—and I'm glad I did. Don't be afraid to play with point of view at the first-draft stage and see which you really like best. Play, and then choose which one tells your story the way you want it told.

Writing Description That Even You Will Want to Read

I confess. I'm a skimmer.

When I'm faced with a lengthy passage of description in a novel, I skim over it and hurry to the more exciting bits, like the action or dialogue. I'm sure that the parts I have skipped are very well written but I'm a hurry-up reader, and when a plot is really racing along, I don't like to slow down. So, how do you put all the details in the story that you want and still keep readers like me interested?

You need to sneak the description in by avoiding those long paragraphs that bring the action to a halt. Here are three things to keep in mind when you want to write description:

- keep it short,
- keep it personal,
- keep it specific.

Keep it short

Look at the series novels for young readers today. The paragraphs are short, lots of dialogue fills the pages, and there is a lot of reader-friendly white paper showing on the page. Dickensian-length paragraphs and sentences are things of the past for popular fiction. Even a look at *The Golden Compass*, a lengthy novel that has a readership of all ages, will show you page after page of paragraphs no more than three to five sentences long. This book is also a great example of a story set in an imaginary *when* that the writer brings to vivid life. Whether your story is set in the now, or the future, or the past, weaving the description into your narrative in short bites is still a good idea.

Keep it personal

If your character walks into a club before it opens for the public, don't stop her at the door to survey the scene and then itemize what she sees for the reader. *Bring the reader into the room with her, and build the details one by one.* Her shoes stick to gobs of something she doesn't want to investigate too closely. She's in a town that hasn't bought into the no-smoking bylaws of the larger cities yet, so she's assaulted by the smell of stale cigarette smoke and the sight of overflowing ashtrays on beer-puddled tables. Keep her moving, thinking about the questions she's going to ask the bartender, worrying about the old man in the corner who is glaring at her, and wishing she hadn't worn white.

Remember, too, that every time you use this technique, you are also building the picture of the character who is reacting to the setting. What if your character, hit by the smell of smoke and spilled beer, takes a deep satisfying lungful and embraces a brief memory of an all-night party where she met her first love. What if, instead of being disgusted when her shoes stick to the floor, she remembers that she rushed out of the house without cleaning up her two-year-old's spilled cereal and that her kitchen floor is going to feel just like this when she gets home. Different characters, different reactions, same disgusting club.

Keep it specific

This is good advice, but it can be dangerous, too. Yes, we need to know that Jim is six feet six inches tall and weighs less than 190 pounds, because in the story he needs to use his height and build to crawl down a narrow shaft to save his buddy's life. But give the reader the information without the numbers, or it sounds like a narrator "factoid," rather than part of the story. "I thought I was tall until I met Jim. If we'd ever had the chance to stand back to back, the top of my head wouldn't have touched his bony shoulder blades. But I never saw him take an awkward step. He flowed from place to place like the long drink of water he seemed to be, head always bowed to avoid banging it on door frames and light fixtures."

"Keep it specific" also means losing words like: beautiful, nice, ugly, pretty, etc. If the food was nice, make our mouths water with the tangy crunch of the apple and the salty bite of the cheese—but only if it's important to the plot. Otherwise, skip to, "After dinner, he ..." If the woman's outfit was awful, tell us how the three shades of purple she wore reminded you of the rotten grapes you'd thrown out that morning and how you could almost see the fruit flies circling her shoulders.

In dialogue, however, those words may be perfectly fine. People rarely give detailed descriptions in dialogue, because that's not how people talk. They will say that they saw the ugliest purple dress in the world or that they had a nice dinner with their friends. When you, the author, have the job of bringing a place or a person to life, that's when you need those specific details.

Do a little homework: reread a part of the novel you are currently reading, and see how that author handles description. Watch for the moments when you skim and then slow down—and find out why. Elmore Leonard, author of the novel *Get Shorty*, gets right to the point on the topic of description: "Don't go into great detail describing places and things, unless you are Margaret Atwood."

Watch the Was's and Is's

Here's what happens when an author uses the *was* voice in a scene.

A blur in green and brown, with a sword that raised to strike him, was seen by Wyatt. Instinctively, Wyatt's sword was swung up in one swift move and was stopping the downward slash of his attacker's blade. The clang of the metal was reverberating to his shoulders. Another wild swing was blocked by him as he was bracing himself.

The following is the way the author actually wrote it:

Wyatt whirled around to see a blur in green and brown, sword raised, moving to strike him. Instinctively, Wyatt swung his sword up in one swift move and stopped the downward slash of his attacker's blade. His shoulders reverberated with the clang of the metal. He braced himself and blocked another wild swing.

What a difference! The first version loses all the power of the action verbs. The action is taken away from the main character (MC) and he becomes someone to whom the action happens. With the *was*'s there, the MC seems to be standing by the action rather than involved in it. That's not what MCs are about. Your writing needs to put the power where it belongs.

Passive voice is a great drainer of power, not just from your MC but from your writing as well. Good writing has a rhythm that sets up the reader for the next thought and then the next. You want your writing to pull the reader along in spite of herself. She just has to read the next paragraph, and the next … Read the next four sentences aloud, and see if you can hear the difference. Which ones have the page-turning beat?

1. He was stared at by the woman with ice eyes. This time the sword wasn't shivering, Wyatt was.

2. The woman stared at him with ice eyes. This time the sword didn't shiver, Wyatt did

1. Wyatt's grip on Peter's hand was released. "Thank you, Peter … um … both of you. I'll do my best." Wyatt's shaking legs were forced to move forward, as he was walking out of the tent and was straightening his shoulders. His hand was resting on the hilt of his sword, and he was muttering, "I'll do my best not to get killed."

2. Wyatt released his grip on Peter's hand. "Thank you, Peter ... um ... both of you. I'll do my best." Wyatt walked out of the tent, straightened his shoulders, and forced his shaking legs to move forward. He rested his hand on the hilt of the sword and muttered, "I'll do my best not to get killed."

You're right; the second quotes are the ones that ended the chapters. The writer wants to make the reader turn the page, and stronger verbs can help make that happen.

Editing for Passive Tense

Using your spelling and grammar checker is a good way to catch passive sentences. Two options help here.

1. With the grammar option on, check that you want readability scores at the end of your check. These scores include the percentage of your sentences that are passive. See if you can keep this percentage below 10 percent. Remember that it's nearly impossible to avoid using *was* or *is* in dialogue or in a person's thoughts, so leave them there. "Helen is a real pain in the neck" is not improved by writing "Helen pains my neck."

2. When you set up your grammar settings, make sure that you have a check mark beside passive sentences. When your grammar check is running, it will pick up passive sentences and offer you an option to change them to active tense.

Another step in eliminating *was* and *is* is by getting rid of the words: *there were, it was, here is,* and variations of those three, at the beginnings of sentences. You rarely need to begin a sentence with any combination of those words. For example: *There was a platoon of soldiers hiding in the woods* becomes *A platoon of soldiers hid in the woods.*

Let's look at some sentences written in passive tense and see how they can be turned around. In both of the following examples, the sentence is strengthened by putting the character at the beginning and letting him or her do something active.

The box was opened by Jill.
Jill opened the box.

The cliff was climbed by Eric.
Eric climbed the cliff.

If the sentence is written in passive voice, put the person who does the action at the beginning of the sentence and rewrite the sentence without the *was* or *is*.

Watch for sentences where an adjective follows a *was* or *is*. These sentences desperately need action and some vivid description. Here are a couple of examples:

Simca was happy.
Simca hugged her sister and laughed out loud.

Lee was sad.
Lee took a shuddering breath and pushed back a sob. No one was going to see her cry—ever.

Watch out for the words *was* and *is* and their companions *were, are* and *be,* and, except for dialogue or thoughts, try to keep them to a minimum in your writing. Your writing will benefit by being more active, vivid, and compelling to read.

Seven Editing Questions and Why You Need to Ask Them

Writers rarely like to revise their work, but it is a reality of the writing process and is actually more important than the writing itself. Without it, writers can't realize the true potential of the story or novel they originally envisioned. Without it, a story will never be published. Here are seven self-editing questions to ask, as you begin revisions on your story or novel.

1.   Where does the story really begin?

Reread the first two to three pages of your story very carefully. When does the action really start? A major fault with many first drafts (mine included!) is that there is too much background material at the beginning, before the conflict is introduced and the characters finally take over the story. In my case, I can almost bet that my story doesn't really begin until about halfway down page three, so out go the first two pages. If the material I have cut contains information the reader needs to know, I find ways later, through dialogue or thoughts of my characters, to get the information to the reader. My later insertions are never as long as those original two and a half pages, and the pace of the story gains needed speed.

2.   Is this adverb necessary?

Chances are, if you are using a lot of adverbs, you are telling and not showing. Think about the character that has just won the lottery. Rather than have her yell hurray "joyfully," why not have her jump up and down screaming so loudly that her cat runs under the bed in terror and it takes her twenty minutes to get it out. Maybe you can have her run to her closet and throw all of her old clothes in the garbage, while blasting "If I Had a Million Dollars" on her CD player. Both of those pictures *show* how the character reacts, instead of *telling*, and they are certainly livelier than the word "joyfully."

3.   Is this adjective doing its job?

You need to replace empty adjectives, such as *amazing, interesting, exciting, awful, ugly, beautiful, nice, scary,* with sensory details that bring to life what you are describing. Find places to get the readers' senses working; it means you are making the story real for them.

4.   Whose problem is it?

Your main character has the problem; your main character needs to solve it. Make sure that your protagonist remains the chief actor in the story and doesn't become solely the reactor to another character's influence. Sometimes, in longer pieces, characters other than your MC can start to steal your attention and your imagination; this can be especially true of villains and comical sidekicks. Be careful that these characters don't become so charming that they threaten to steal the book from your hero or heroine.

5.   Are the grammar and spelling perfect?

Yes, I mean *perfect*. The most that an editor needs to read of a short story in order to make a decision is approximately three paragraphs; a novel might get three pages. If that's the only chance you have, don't blow it by showing your lack of ability in spelling and grammar. Of course, publishers have people whose job it is to make sure that the copy they publish is correct in every way, but there's no way they're going to waste that person's time on writers who haven't bothered to do their best the first time.

6.   Have I read my story out loud?

One of your best proofreading tools is the sound of your own voice. Reading your story aloud is a great way to find awkward or incomplete sentences, clumsy phrasing, and inconsistencies in verb tenses and pronoun agreement. If you hesitate when you are reading, or if you have to reread a sentence or phrase, then that's a section of your story that needs a rewrite.

7.   Have I applied the Stephen King rule?

Stephen King concludes his autobiography, *On Writing: A Memoir of the Craft*, with an editing exercise. He shows you the first draft of a story he has written and then shows it again full of his cross-outs, inserts, and editing marks. He explains his edits and why he makes the choices he does. King's revision rule is: "Second Draft = First Draft - 10 percent." We have a tendency, as writers, to believe that every word we write is precious, and we are very reluctant to cut our material—after all, we remember how hard it was to get it down on paper the first time. However, editing is about making our prose lean, and exciting, and compelling enough to keep the reader turning pages. See what you can do with ten percent fewer words.

Consider revision a reward. Remember that, if you are revising, you have finished a project—how great is that? Try these seven questions to kick-start your editing and begin your pursuit of a great final product.

Connecting With Other Writers

It's never too early to seek out the company of other writers. Look through the coming events brochures at your local library and see if they have any authors coming to visit. Or check with your school librarian. There may be an author coming to visit your school who isn't going to speak to your grade. See if you can get to see him or her anyway. Writers need to hear from other writers. It's a lonely occupation, and it makes a difference to find out that professional authors have the same struggles, the same weird moments when characters seem to take over the keyboard, and the same rejections from publishers.

Authors often tour, visiting libraries and schools. Check the Web sites of your favorite authors (or their publishers) and see when they might be in your area. Bookstores sometimes have authors come in for signings or to do book talks. If you have a university in your area, check if it has a writer-in-residence who offers public lectures or readings or if any writers are coming to visit.

And don't worry if the authors that are visiting your neighborhood don't write the same kinds of stories or poems that you do. They all have something to teach you, or a way to inspire you, or a great anecdote that makes you want to run to the keyboard and get your novel, story, or poem going again.

Writers' organizations are other great resources for writers. For whatever genre of writing you prefer to write, there will be an organization of like-minded writers. Google what interests you, and you'll find what you're looking for. Here is a sample list for you to explore. Many have how-to articles and information available on their sites to nonmembers. They all offer conferences, and many have courses or workshops offered online.

- Mystery Writers of America: www.mysterywriters.org
- Crime Writers of Canada: www.crimewriterscanada.com
- Sisters in Crime: www.sistersincrime.org
- Science Fiction and Fantasy Writers of America: www.sfwa.org
- SF Canada: www.sfcanada.ca
- Horror: www.horror.org
- Romance Writers of America: www.rwanational.org
- Christian Writers: www.christianwriters.com
- Canadian Society of Canadian Authors, Illustrators and Performers: www.canscaip.ca
- Society of Children's Book Writers and Illustrators: www.scbwi.org
- Write 4 Kids: www.write4kids.com

Your local library can also be a source of magazines that are written especially for writers. Among them are *Writer's Digest, The Writer,* and *Writer's Journal.* These magazines feature regular columns on poetry, magazine writing, short story and novel writing, and writing for film and television. Bookstores will carry these titles, too, but the library is cheaper.

Look around your classes or among your friends, and think about forming a writers' group of your own. There are many advantages to knowing that you are going to meet your friends every month to talk about writing—not the least of which is that you have to do some writing before you see them the next time. There's nothing like a deadline to help get the work done. Groups do need ground rules, so think about how to organize and guide the discussion and criticism for the benefit of all the members. Take turns chairing the meetings, so that everyone takes a share of the load, and don't forget to bring some goodies to eat. An evening spent with fellow writers should be a treat in every way.

Writing is a solitary occupation, so find ways to break out and meet people who do what you do. Join or create a writers' group, or find a way to meet a writer. Get connected, and then go back to the writing feeling refreshed and ready for wonderful new challenges.

Inspiration: Be Ready For It!

I'm not going to talk about where to find inspiration, but, rather, how to be ready to use it when it arrives. Things come along every day that inspire, that are great ideas for stories, novels, or poems. But what do you need to fulfill the latter part of the definition? What do you need to make the art?

> **INSPIRATION**
> Definition: Stimulus to do creative work
> *Something that stimulates the human mind to creative thought or to the making of art.*
> *Encarta Dictionary*: English (North America)

The first step you need to take is to be a working writer. I don't mean that you have to be at your computer pounding on the keys all day. Working as a writer can mean other things as well, especially keeping full your own personal resource of memories and words that provide the raw materials for your creation.

Let me ask you: When you're out in the world, are you open to new sights and sounds? Do you take a moment to look at the sunset or sunrise, to listen to the sounds of your neighborhood—radios, leaf blowers, children playing, dogs barking, airplanes overhead, a motorcycle a few blocks away? Where else are you going to get the vivid details to paint the picture that your inspiration suggests?

Do you listen to people—not just to your own circle of friends and family, but to people on the bus or at work? What are their speech rhythms and patterns like? Do their voices go up at the ends of sentences? Perhaps they use a lot of technical jargon, or catchphrases like "you know," or "like," or "right." Do they talk about their kids all the time or complain about the boss? All of these details make up the palette from which you create your word pictures—your stories and poems.

At a recent workshop, participants heard from a woman who had lots of story ideas. She shared some with us, and they were wonderful. She was definitely inspired and had the tools to create wonderful pictures for her listeners. She was also a self-confessed procrastinator. What a shame! She wanted to be a writer very much but had never made her dream come true, because she kept putting it off. Do you keep saying that you'll write that story or novel "someday"? Make that someday *now*.

Get out a calendar and set a due date for your finished product. Log your activities, hour by hour, for a week. Find out where you can take the time to get your writing done. Do you need to watch all those TV shows when they're on? Can you record them and watch them some other time? Having a big chunk of time for writing is wonderful, but it can be very intimidating to fill with constructive work, especially if you're not used to it. Chipping away at a project a little at a time is a great solution and also helps you develop the habit of sitting at the keyboard and writing every day.

Make sure you keep reading, too. Immerse yourself in someone else's writing. Read the words aloud to hear the rhythms and to understand how the author keeps the action moving with sentence variety. Expand your vocabulary. Look up words the author uses that you don't know. When you are writing your story and looking for just the right word, you'll have it at your fingertips. Vary your reading, so that you read in different genres and forms: mystery, sci-fi, literary, romance, poetry, adventure, or short stories. When inspiration strikes, you can take your ideas and frame them in the form and style of writing that serves them best.

Lastly, write even when you're not inspired. Athletes practise when it's not race day, and writers need to write even when there's no deadline or no real inspiration. Writing "muscles" need to be kept in trim, too. You need to find words and put them together with depth of meaning and in a way that grabs a reader. This needs to be a daily habit, not just an intermittent exercise that you take on when the mood strikes you.

Keeping a daily journal is one way to strengthen those muscles and keep them flexed. Another is to play with words whenever you can. Take a line from a song you like, and use that to start a story or a poem. Describe what you see out of your window, or write from a different point of view, such as that of your baseball cap, or your backpack, or your running shoes, or your alarm clock.

Who knows? You may be inspired. And when you are, you'll have all the tools you need to create your work of art.

Beat Writer's Block by Playing Your Cards Right

Some writers say that there is no such thing as writer's block. Others believe that it is a real monster lying in wait to turn your creativity to stone just when you need it the most. I believe that the writer's block monster is really out there, but I also believe that he can be beaten. The trick is to challenge him to a duel, the way the TV animé heroes duel their opponents, and to summon some monster and magic cards of your own. Let's take a few out of the writer's deck and see what they can do.

The Time-to-Move-On Card

Play this card if the story is really dead. Maybe you can't make any progress on this story because the idea simply wasn't strong enough in the first place. Don't feel guilty—just move on.

The What-If Magic Card

Maybe you've been limiting your character's options. Play "what if" for a while, and see what happens. What if X breaks his leg right now in your story? What if the teddy bear Y got for her birthday grants her three wishes? What if Z's gel pens suddenly begin to write flawless French? What if … now you try.

The Manuscript-Reborn Card

If your current project is feeling like it's a failure, put it away. Then pull out something you filed away in the past. Sometimes reading an old piece of writing can give you a real lift. You remember how good a writer you are or see an angle to develop on a story that you thought was finished. There's nothing like a boost to your self-confidence to break up a bad case of writer's block.

The Reality-Check Card

This is the hardest card to play and has the highest attack value, which means you have to pay a price to play it. The price is self-examination. Is the reason you can't write that it's just hard work facing the blank screen/page, and you're simply not tough enough to sit there until the work is done? If you believe that you truly have the attack points and attitude that you need, then retire this card to the graveyard, and play the next one.

The Play-Until-It-Works Card

Did I say "play"? Sure.

Sometimes the idea of taking a risk is overwhelmed by the fear of failure, and you stop trying, or you're afraid to begin. You may have a lot invested in this new project, and you really want to make it work. The pressure to succeed can choke the writing.

This is where play comes in. I mean, you can't fail if you are just playing, right? Grab a book or magazine and, with your eyes closed, put a finger on the page. Now write down the word you're pointing to. Do it three times, or as many times as you need until you find a connection—no matter how weird—and start writing. This technique accounts for a story of mine called "Sherlock Holmes and the Lonely Spider". I admit it's not a great story, but it got me hitting the keyboard again and producing words. After all, if I could turn that combination into a story, I should have no problem with an idea that actually makes sense.

The You're-Not-Alone Card

Play this card and remember that you're not the first, nor will you be the last, writer to be stopped by writer's block. Remember, too, that the good ones—like you—got through it and kept on writing. To succeed, they played the next card.

The Perseverance Card

Face the monster down with your determination and talent, and he'll back away. Never make him more important than the writing. You have a story to tell, and you need to keep the seat of your pants applied to the chair and write it. And if you don't? Well, it's hard to succeed when you're walking away from your goal.

Lawrence Kasdan wrote that, "[being] a writer is like having homework for the rest of your life." If you're tough enough or crazy enough to commit yourself to that kind of life, then you can defeat whatever monster is trying to take it away from you.

Stack your deck with perseverance, playfulness, a dose of reality and some well-deserved praise, and make the writer's block monster disappear. Remember, you have a lifetime of homework to do, and the time to start is now.

Keeping the Writer in You Motivated

Here are eight tricks, thoughts, and suggestions for keeping you in creative gear, when the demands of the rest of your life make that difficult.

- *Rethink what you really need to be a writer.* At the most basic level, you need a pencil and paper and the will to apply one to the other for a period of time. You don't need a computer to write the first draft of anything. If you need it, then you have to be in the same room with it. And that means you can't write anywhere else or in any other way. Think about how limiting that is. When time to write is so scarce, limiting yourself to *one* writing location can make it nearly impossible to write at all.

- *Promise yourself writing time, and make a space for it in your life every day.* This can be a difficult promise to keep, but it can be done. I know this may be a challenge, but consider setting the alarm for an earlier time and hitting the page before the rest of your day begins to crowd in. Dorothea Brande, author of *Becoming a Writer,* recommends a half-hour of writing in the morning, right after you wake up and before you talk to anyone or even read.

- *Give yourself a twenty-minute gift of writing time.* Don't tell yourself that there's no point in starting because you don't have a clear three hours in which to write. Inspiration will find you whether you're on the bus or waiting for the movie to start or the dentist to call you in. If you're meeting a friend for coffee, get there twenty minutes early and take your notebook. Those twenty-minute blocks add up, and, think about it, writing for twenty minutes is better than not writing at all.

- *Set a goal.* You might find that a weekly one works best. You have seven days to write five pages or two thousand words. If you're a natural-born procrastinator, you need to break your goal down into small daily chunks. And be easy on yourself if you don't make every personal writing deadline. Remember, one chocolate bar doesn't end a diet. You have a lot in your life right now. Congratulate yourself on what you did do, because each page you filled got you closer to your goal. And there's always another day, or another twenty-minute gift you can give to yourself.

- *Never stop thinking of yourself as a writer.* When you wake up, think about what you will do for the writer today—eavesdrop on a conversation and record one really good line of dialogue? Read great writing? Write down three unrelated words and think of a story that will connect them? Add a paragraph to your current piece? Do some research? Edit a page? Buy a new pencil? Use the word *writer* to define yourself, and you will honor your commitment to the writer, as you do to the friend, parent, sibling, teacher, boss, and co-worker who also need your attention every day.

- ***Lose the perfectionist.*** Give yourself permission to write a first draft that is a mess. Just get the words down. They don't have to be the words that end up in the final story. That's what second drafts are for—and thirds! Follow the advice of Ms. Frizzle, of *The Magic School Bus*: "Take chances, make mistakes, and get messy."

- ***Have more than one story or poem on the go.*** That way, you will always have something to write, even if one idea is dead, or your inspiration for it is. Remember, too, that you don't have to write a story or a poem in order. If you have a clear idea of how a scene or description or a stanza will work later on, write it now and connect it later. But write.

- ***The best advice is last. Start now!***

Last Words

My last words are an invitation. Visit my Web site, say "hello," ask questions, or drop off a paragraph or two of your story for me to read. I'd love to know how your writing projects are progressing and how you're enjoying the writing process.

I hope you haven't just read the book, but instead have played with some of the exercises and are now working on a writing project that really excites you. Let me know what you liked about the book, what you didn't like, and what you'd like to see in the next edition. If revisions don't end up in print, I can always add chapters or comments on topics of your choice on the Web site. That's what it's for.

I wish you all the best in your writing and hope that you enjoy being a writer so much that you never stop. I don't plan to—ever!

Yours,

Heather

REFERENCES

Brande, Dorothea. *Becoming a Writer.* New York, New York: Harcourt, Brace & Company, 1934.

Frey, James N. *The Key: How to Write Damn Good Fiction Using the Power of Myth.* New York, New York: St. Martin's Press, 2000.

Kasdan, Lawrence, and George Lucas. *The Return of the Jedi.* 1983.

King, Stephen. *On Writing: A Memoir of the Craft.* New York, New York: Pocket Books, 2000.

Kurtzman, Alex, Roberto Orci, and John Rogers. *Transformers.* 2007.

Lee, Harper. *To Kill a Mockingbird.* New York, New York: Harper Collins, 1960.

Leonard, Elmore. *Get Shorty.* New York, New York: Bantam Books, 2000.

Lucas, George. *Star Wars.* 1977

Paolini, Christopher. *Eragon.* New York, New York: Alfred A. Knopf, 2003.

Pullman, Philip. *The Golden Compass.* New York, New York: Alfred. A. Knopf, 1995.

Rowling, J. K. *Harry Potter and the Philosopher's Stone.* New York, New York: Scholastic, 1998.

Seuss, Dr. *How the Grinch Stole Christmas*. New York, New York: Random House, 1957.

The Writer. Milwaukee, Wisconsin: Kalmbach Publishing Company.

Tolkien, J. R. R. *The Fellowship of the Ring.* New York, New York: Mariner Books, 1999.

Vogler, Christopher. *The Writer's Journey: Mythic Structure for Writers, 3ʳᵈ Edition.* Studio City, California: Michael Wiese Productions, 2007.

Wendkos, Gina. *The Princess Diaries*. 2001.

Writer's Digest. Cincinnati, Ohio: F & W Media.

Writer's Journal. Perham, Minnesota: Val-Tech Media.